wirework

Using wire for beautiful home decoration

Karin Hossack
Photography by Michelle Garrett

southwater

This edition published by Southwater

Southwater is an imprint of
Anness Publishing Limited
Hermes House
88–89 Blackfriars Road
London SE1 8HA
tel. 020 7401 2077
fax. 020 7633 9499

Distributed in the UK by
The Manning Partnership
251-253 London Road East
Batheaston
Bath BA1 7RL
UK
tel. (0044) 01225 852 727
fax. (0044) 01225 852 852

Distributed in the USA by
Anness Publishing Inc.
27 West 20th Street
Suite 504
New York NY10011
USA
tel. 212   807 6739
fax. 212 807 6813

Distributed in Australia by
Sandstone Publishing
Unit 1, 360 Norton Street
Leichhardt
New South Wales 2040
Australia
tel. 02 9560 7888
fax. 02 9560 7488

1 3 5 7 9 10 8 6 4 2

Publisher: Joanna Lorenz
Editor: Charlotte Berman
Designer: Lilian Lindblom
Step Photographer: Rodney Forte
Illustrators: Madeleine David and Robert Highton
Production: Steve Lang

PUBLISHER'S NOTE
FOR SAFETY, PROTECTIVE GLOVES SHOULD BE WORN WHEN USING WIRE THAT HAS
SHARP EDGES, AND NAKED FLAMES SHOULD NEVER BE LEFT UNATTENDED.

CONTENTS

INTRODUCTION

Wire has been used for decorative purposes from as far back as 3000BC, and for domestic objects since the 10th century, but due to the corrodible nature of iron very few examples of wirework from the early 19th century and before still exist. Any old pieces that you are lucky enough to come across may well be slightly mis-shapen due to their years of use as a treasured household device.

Wirework reached its peak at the turn of the 20th century. By this time tinning and black-japanning had become popular ways of protecting the wireworker's craft, and items ranging from the simple whisk to large garden structures were readily available. However, the expansion of plastic manufacturing, an even more versatile material, brought about the demise of wirework. Since then the art of creating items from wire has moved from the domestic arena into the area of fine art, but recently there has been a resurgence in interest in all areas, as contemporary artists and amateur enthusiasts alike recognise that not only is wire cheap and readily available, but it also has the potential to be transformed into objects of great beauty and strength.

The projects in this book include items for all around the house and garden, such as a simple Flower Fly Swatter, Mesh Place Mat and handy Garden Drinks Carrier. The Materials section shows just how many varieties of wire can be found around the home, while the Basic Techniques section reveals all the tricks of the trade you will need in order to create your own wirework pieces.

Deborah Barker

FLOWER FLY SWATTER

This unusual fly swat is simple to make and extremely effective. It is designed to resemble a giant flower, so if you're lucky enough not to have to use it much, at least it won't be an eyesore in the kitchen.

YOU WILL NEED
wire coat hanger
wire cutters
pliers
broom handle
tape measure
2.5 cm/1 in diameter wooden ball
pencil
plastic mesh
scissors
cotton knitting yarn
needle

1 Cut the hook off a wire coat hanger and straighten the wire. Bend the top end of the wire through 90°. Then, using a broom handle, form a loop in the end and trim off the excess wire. Use the diagram at the back of the book as a guide.

2 Measure down 45 cm/18 in from the top and bend another 90° angle. Turn this end around the broom handle twice to make a double loop, then bend at 90° again and cut off, leaving a 4 cm/1½ in length parallel with the stem.

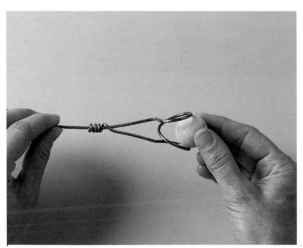

3 Twist the end of the wire around the stem. Spread the double loop open and insert the wooden ball.

4 Enlarge the template at the back of the book, trace on to plastic mesh, and cut out. Centre the top loop on the splat and oversew firmly with cotton yarn.

SPIRAL NAPKIN HOLDERS

Simple copper coils with a random sprinkling of bright beads make attractive napkin rings for a special occasion. If you are designing a buffet table setting for a larger party, you can scale up the same design to make a holder for paper napkins.

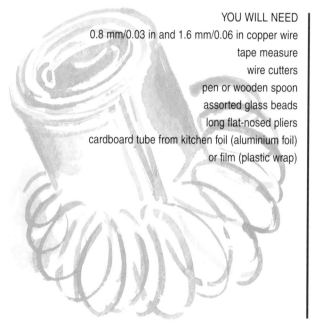

YOU WILL NEED
0.8 mm/0.03 in and 1.6 mm/0.06 in copper wire
tape measure
wire cutters
pen or wooden spoon
assorted glass beads
long flat-nosed pliers
cardboard tube from kitchen foil (aluminium foil)
or film (plastic wrap)

1 Cut a 1 m/3 ft length of 0.8 mm/0.03 in copper wire and wind it on to a pen or the handle of a wooden spoon. As you form each loop, add a few small glass beads in assorted colours.

2 Form 18 coils to make a tight spring, then slide it off the pen or wooden spoon. Twist the two wire ends tightly together using pliers.

3 Add a small bead and pull the ends of the wire around it to secure.

▶

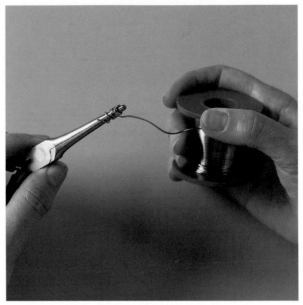

4 To make a larger ring, use 1.6 mm/0.06 in copper wire and larger beads. Form the coils around a cardboard tube, such as the inside of a roll of kitchen foil (aluminium foil) or film (plastic wrap).

5 Make a small tight coil of 0.8 mm/0.03 in copper wire using long flat-nosed pliers and slide it over both ends of the spring.

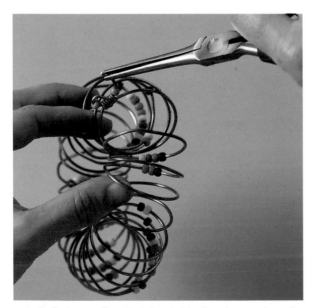

6 Pull the small coil tight. Add a bead to each end of the large spring and loop the ends of the wire over the bead to secure it.

Above: You could choose beads to match the colour of the napkins, or even the table decorations.

WINDOW BOX EDGING

Galvanized wire is ideal for the garden, as it will not rust when exposed to the elements. This pretty repeating heart pattern can be used to edge a window box or a flower pot, or even, if you make enough, to add an orderly trimming to an unruly garden border.

YOU WILL NEED
paper
felt-tipped pen
1.6 mm/0.06 in galvanized wire
tape measure
wire cutters
flat-nosed pliers

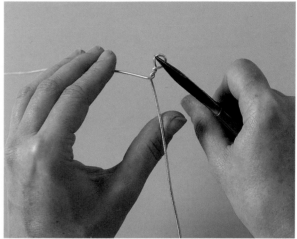

1 Scale up the template at the back of the book to a height of 15 cm/6 in as a guide for bending the wire. Cut a 43 cm/17 in length of galvanized wire and bend it in half. Holding the central loop with pliers, twist the two ends around each other twice.

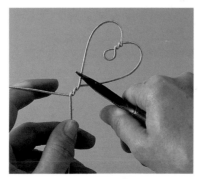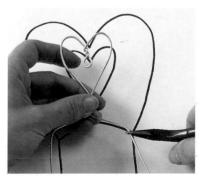

2 Bend the two tails around the loop to form a small heart shape, using the template as a guide. Cross the wires at the bottom of the heart.

3 Hold the heart shape with pliers just above the crossing point and twist the two free ends around three times.

4 Bend the two free ends out and down, following the template.

▶

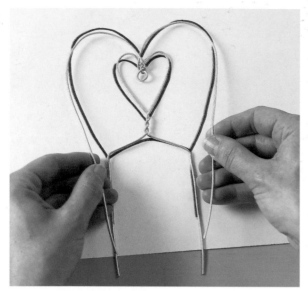

5 Cut a 48 cm/19 in length of wire, bend in half as before and loop the centre over the twisted loop in the small heart shape. Use pliers to flatten the loop, then bend the outer wires down following the template.

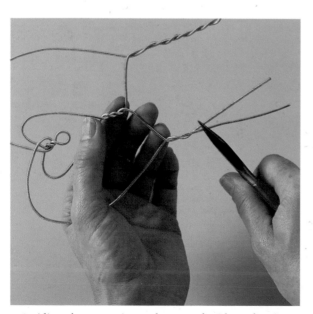

6 Align the two wire ends on each side and twist them tightly together. Use wire cutters to even up the lengths of wire at the bottom of the twists.

CLASSIC CANDLESTICKS

Aluminium wire is fun to work with as it is light and easy to bend, but a group of these twisted candlesticks makes a substantial centrepiece.

YOU WILL NEED
3 mm/0.11 in and 1.6 mm/0.06 in aluminium wire
tape measure
wire cutters
0.8 mm/0.03 in coloured copper wire
round-nosed jewellery pliers
three glass beads
candle
two pencils

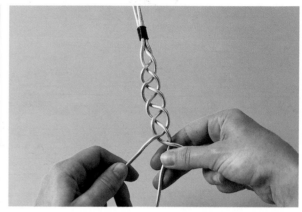

1 Cut three equal lengths of of 3 mm/0.11 in aluminium wire. These should be 45 cm/18 in for the small, 50 cm/20 in for the medium or 55 cm/22 in for the tall candlestick. Bind the three pieces together 10 cm/4 in from the top using coloured copper wire, then plait (braid) them together.

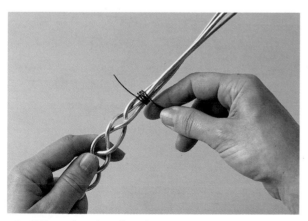

2 When the plait (braid) measures 10 cm/4 in, 15 cm/6 in or 18 cm/7 in, depending on the size you are making, bind the three pieces together with coloured wire as at the top.

3 Separate the three wires beneath the binding and shape into legs, bending each wire up and then down to make a double curve. Use round-nosed pliers to curl each end into a loop, which must be equal in height, and add a bead.

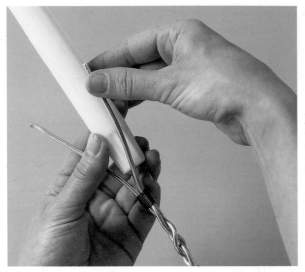

4 Open out the wires at the top of the candlestick. Position a candle on the wires and mould them around it.

5 Cut a 150 cm/59 in length of 1.6 mm/0.06 in aluminium wire and fold it in half. Loop a pencil into each end of the doubled wire and twist it, using the pencils as handles. Cut a 75 cm/30 in length of coloured wire and wind it over the top of the twisted aluminium.

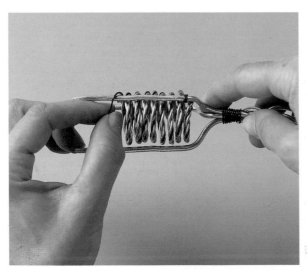

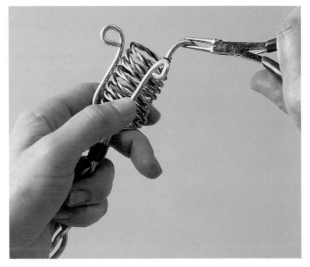

6 Coil a 50 cm/20 in length of the twisted wire gently around the base of the candle, then bind this coil inside the shaped spikes with a few turns of coloured wire at the top and the bottom of each spike.

7 To complete the candlestick, use round-nosed pliers to curl the spikes down into three loops.

PRETTY PLATE EDGING

To turn the plainest plate you can find into something very special use flattened coils to make up the decoration, wired together with a simple overcast wrap to add a subtle touch of colour.

YOU WILL NEED

2 mm/0.08 in aluminium wire

tape measure

wire cutters

30 cm/12 in length of 1 cm/½ in dowel or stiff cardboard tube

26 cm/10¼ in white dinner plate

masking tape

flat-nosed pliers

round pencil

towel or cloth

rolling pin

25 g/1 oz reel of 0.6 mm/0.025 in lilac enamelled aluminium wire

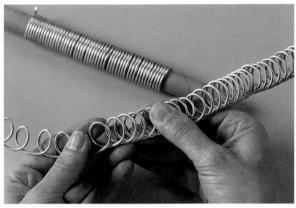

1 Measure and cut a 3 m/10 ft length of 2 mm/ 0.08 in aluminium wire, and wrap it around a piece of 1 cm/½ in dowel. Spread the coil so that the loops are approximately 5 mm/¼ in apart, and flatten it. Working from one end, prise the flattened rings open, leaving a small gap in between each.

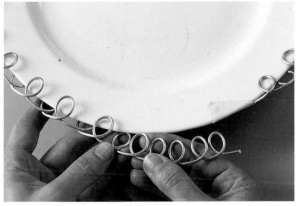

2 Bend the flattened coil into a circle, with the rings facing in. Place it around the edge of the plate and press it firmly into position by pushing one ring under the rim and the next over the top. Use masking tape to hold the end in place as you work. ▶

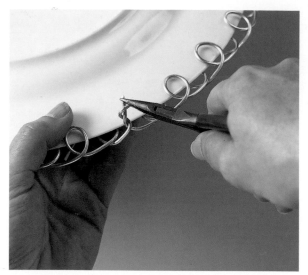

3 Push the last ring under the rim, then turn the plate over. Remove the tape and adjust the spacing of the first and last rings to match the rest. Open out the ends of the wire and twist them together. Press them down flat towards the base of the plate.

4 Measure and cut a 3.6 m/12 ft length of aluminium wire. Coil this around a round pencil and spread the rings out so that there is a 3 mm/⅛ in gap between them. Lay the coil on a towel and use a rolling pin to flatten it.

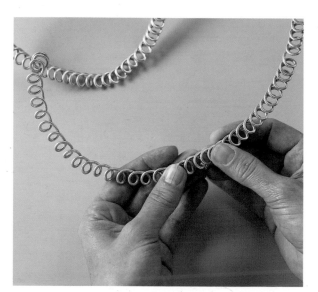

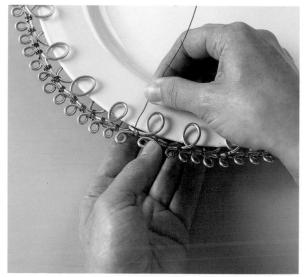

5 Pull the coil apart so that a small gap shows between the edges of the rings, keeping the size of the rings even.

6 With the rings on the outside, position the small coil around the outside edge of the large coil. Bind the two coils together using lilac enamelled aluminium wire. Wrap the fine wire three times around each loop of the small coil and fasten off securely.

FLOWER LAMPSHADE

This charming little shade is decorative rather than functional: you should use a low wattage bulb, but you could hang a few together for maximum effect. The choice of paper is important as it defines the whole nature of the lampshade.

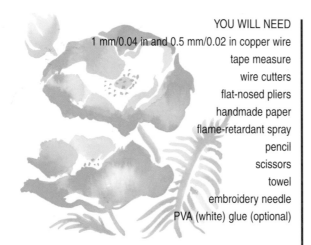

YOU WILL NEED

1 mm/0.04 in and 0.5 mm/0.02 in copper wire
tape measure
wire cutters
flat-nosed pliers
handmade paper
flame-retardant spray
pencil
scissors
towel
embroidery needle
PVA (white) glue (optional)

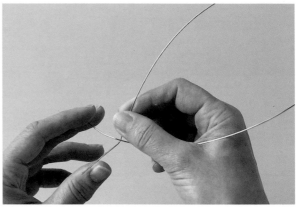

1 Cut a 40 cm/16 in length of 1 mm/0.04 in copper wire. (For a larger flower cut a 50 cm/20 in length.) Twist the two ends together for 1 cm/ ½ in, then pull the loop into a petal shape to match the template at the back of the book.

Above: you can stiffen fine paper if necessary with a coat of diluted PVA (white) glue.

2 Spray the paper with flame-retardant spray. When dry, place the wire petal shape on the paper and draw around it. Cut out the petal, then place it on a towel and use an embroidery needle to punch holes evenly around the edge.

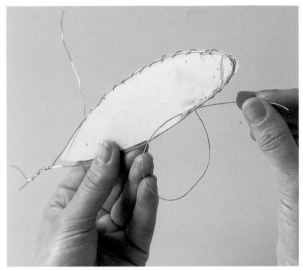

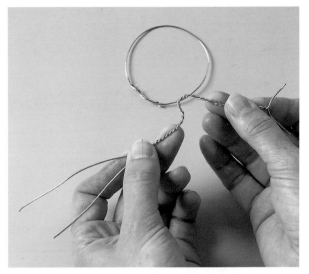

3 Cut a 50 cm/20 in length of 0.5 mm/0.02 in copper wire and fold it in half to mark the centre. Starting at the tip of the petal, thread the wire through the first hole and pull it through as far as the centre mark. Work up one side then the other, sewing the petal to the frame. Twist the ends together and trim off. Make six petals.

4 Cut a 25 cm/10 in length of the thicker wire and form a 6 cm/2¾ in diameter circle. Cut two 10 cm/4 in lengths and twist them together. Form a half-loop in the middle, following the template.

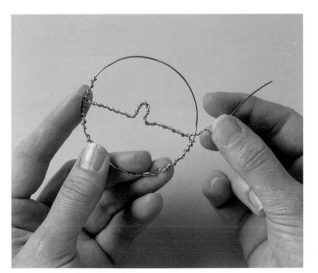

5 Attach the looped rod by twisting the ends around the circle, to form a frame for the petals.

6 Join the petals in a row by threading the finer wire through a punched hole on each side of each petal 4 cm/1½ in from the top, then twisting and trimming the ends. ▶

7 Attach the petals to the circle in the same way, passing the fine wire through the same hole where the petals are joined together. Once all the petals are joined, bend over the tops and splay the bottoms of the petals to shape the flower.

HANGING STRING DISPENSER

An elegantly simple wire cage will ensure that a ball of string is always there when you need it and that it never gets into a tangle. Easy to refill and attractive to look at, it's a useful accessory for the kitchen, workshop or potting shed.

YOU WILL NEED
2 mm/0.08 in and 1 mm/0.04 in galvanized wire
tape measure
wire cutters
pliers
broom handle
ball of string
length of garden cane
pencil

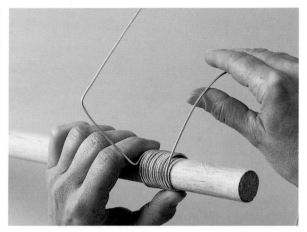

1 Cut a piece of 2 mm/0.08 in galvanized wire 170 cm/67 in long. Bend a right angle about 30 cm/12 in from the end, then make 11 coils in the wire by turning it around a broom handle.

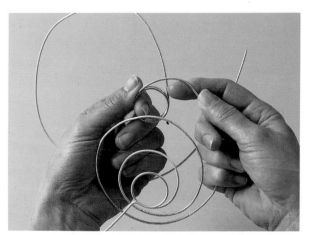

2 Loosen and spread the coils to form a hemisphere large enough to fit loosely around the ball of string.

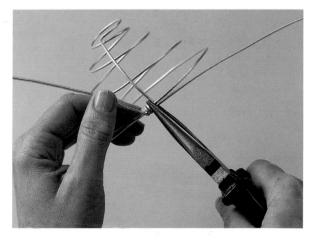

3 Bend the end of the wire down around the hemisphere and use it to bind the last circle closed, leaving enough wire to create the feed loop for the string. ▶

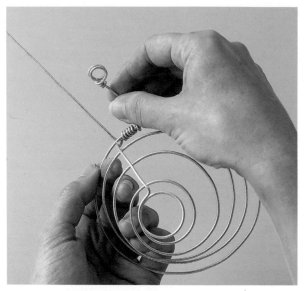

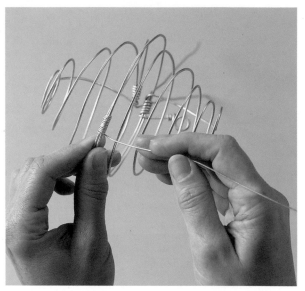

4 To make the loop for the string, wind a double coil around a garden cane about 2.5 cm/1 in along the remaining wire. Twist the end of the wire tightly around the stem and trim.

5 Make a second, matching hemisphere, omitting the string loop. Using 1 mm/0.04 in wire, bind the two halves together on the side opposite the loop and hooks.

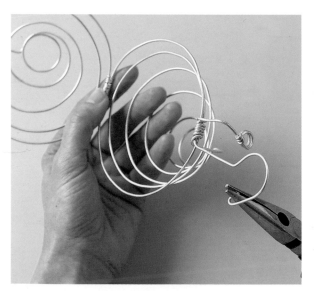

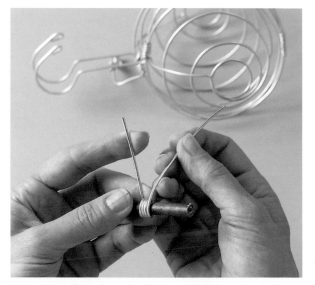

6 On each half, bend the free end of the wire at 90° to the circle and create two matching hanging hooks. Complete each hook with a tight loop at the end.

7 Cut a short length of 2 mm/0.08 in wire and coil it several times around a pencil to make a closing ring for the dispenser. Trim the ends and thread the ring over the hooks to keep the two halves closed.

MESH PLACE MAT

Although it looks intricate, there is nothing more to this colourful tablemat than plain knitting and a simple double crochet stitch. Crystal seed beads add to the glittering effect created when the enamelled wire catches the light.

YOU WILL NEED

50 g/2 oz each of 0.4 mm/0.016 in enamelled copper wire in
burgundy and pink
pair 2.75 mm/size 12/US 2 knitting needles
wire cutters
ruler
2 mm/size 14/B-1 crochet hook
seed beads
sewing needle

1 Using burgundy wire and 2.75 mm/size 12/US 2 knitting needles, loosely cast on 52 stitches. Knit every row until the work measures 22 cm/8½ in.

Above: This striking table mat can be made in any variety of colours that you prefer.

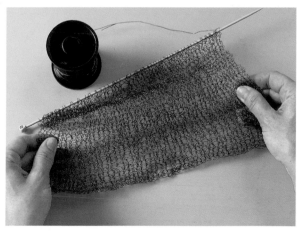

2 When you reach this length, pull the work from the sides and from the top and bottom to stretch the mat out to the final measurement of 23 x 29 cm/ 9 x 11½ in. If necessary, add a few more rows to correct the length, then cast off loosely. ▶

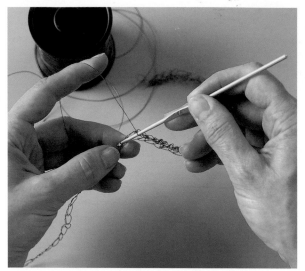

3 Using pink wire and a 2 mm/size 14/B-1 crochet hook, loosely chain crochet 165 stitches. Turn the work, miss 1 chain, then double crochet/ single crochet into every chain. At the end of this length cut the wire, leaving a tail of 2.5 cm/1 in.

4 Thread 82 crystal seed beads on to a length of pink wire.

5 Holding several seed beads in your left hand, work along the edging strip again in double crochet, adding in one seed bead to every other double crochet stitch.

6 Work two more rows in double crochet and cast off. Measure the finished edging around the edge of the mat and stretch evenly if necessary to make it fit. Thread a needle with pink wire. Starting in a corner of the mat, use an overcast stitch to sew on the pink edging.

MONOGRAMMED CLOTHES HANGER

These hangers make lovely gifts, or a charming gesture in a guest's bedroom. The instructions show how to make the hanger itself as well as the decoration, but if you are short of time you can use a ready-made wire hanger and omit the first three steps.

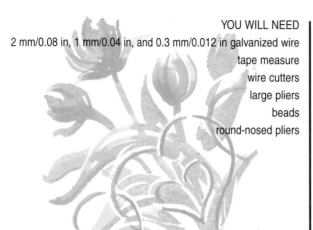

YOU WILL NEED
2 mm/0.08 in, 1 mm/0.04 in, and 0.3 mm/0.012 in galvanized wire
tape measure
wire cutters
large pliers
beads
round-nosed pliers

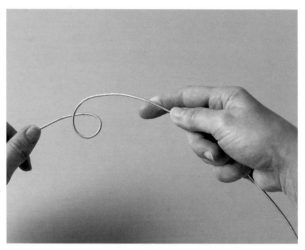

1 Cut a 140 cm/55 in length of 2 mm/0.08 in galvanized wire. Form a loop 25 cm/10 in from one end.

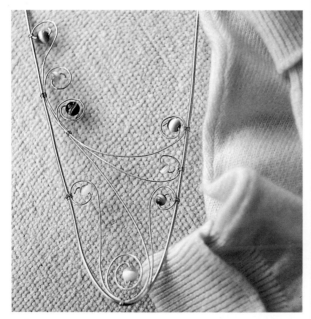

Above: This elegant creation is just as strong as everyday coathangers, as it is made from the same type of wire.

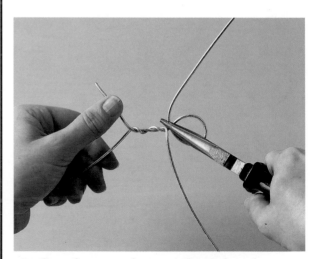

2 Cross the two ends over at the circle and, holding them at the crossing-point with pliers, twist the two ends together for 5 cm/2 in.

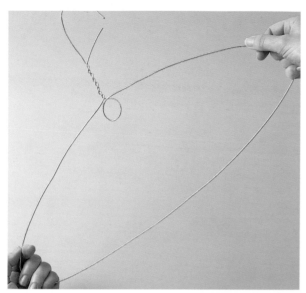

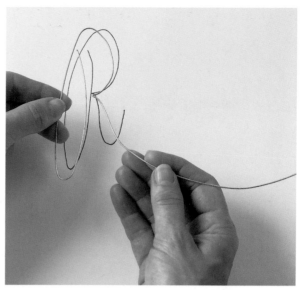

3 Above the twist, trim off the short end and shape the longer end to form the hook. Holding the circle of wire with the hook at the top, pull out the sides to form the hanger shape.

4 Using 1 mm/0.04 in galvanized wire, shape the initial letter for the centre of the hanger following the relevant template from the alphabet at the back of the book.

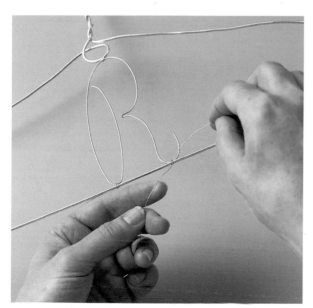

5 Bind the letter to the hanger at the top and bottom using 0.3 mm/0.012 in galvanized wire.

6 With 1 mm/0.04 in wire, make the decorative shapes using the templates at the back of the book as a guide. Thread beads on to the ends of the wires, then twist into shape using round-nosed pliers. ▶

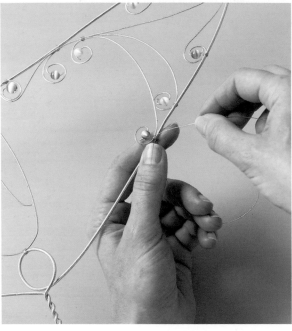

7 Attach the shapes to the main frame in the order
of the numbers shown on the template. Bind
each one to the top and bottom of the hanger, using
fine wire as before.

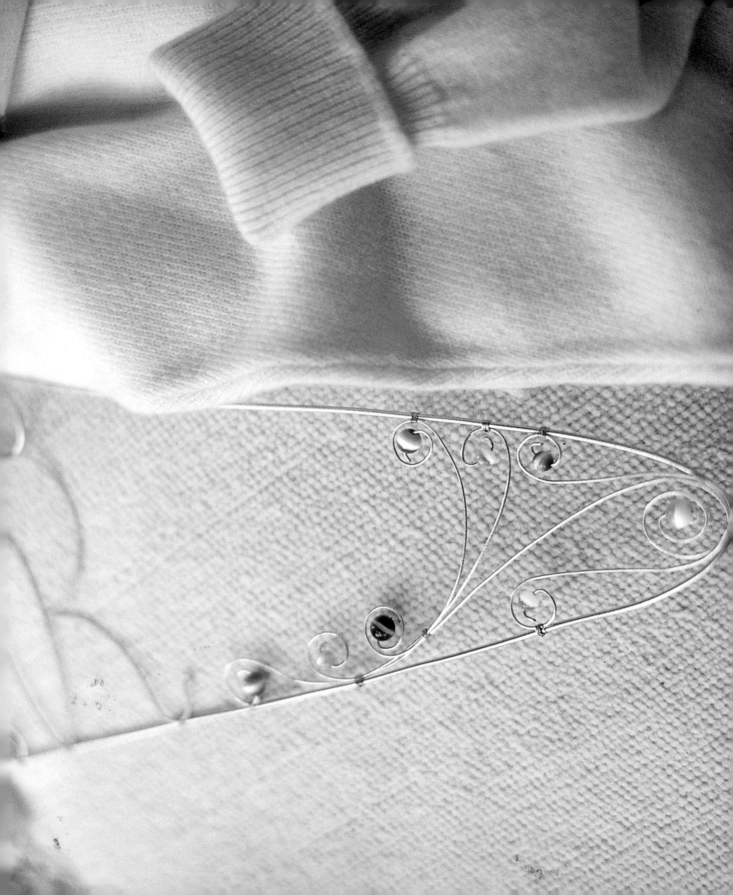

WIRED GLASS LANTERN

*Decorated with a bright net of coloured wire to catch the light, an ordinary preserving jar
makes an ideal holder for a citronella candle to ward off summer insects.*

YOU WILL NEED
glass preserving jar
0.5 mm/0.02 in coloured enamelled copper wire
tape measure
wire cutters
flat-nosed pliers
citronella candle

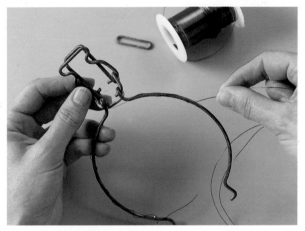

1 Remove the lid of the jar and the metal ring
around the neck. Cut a 2 m/6 ft length of
coloured enamelled copper wire. Beginning at one
open end of the metal ring and leaving a 6 cm/2¾ in
tail, loosely wrap the coloured wire around the metal
ring, making six turns on each side of the catch.

*Above: Decorated preserving jars look great either filled with
dried beans or as a container for scented candles.*

2 Replace the metal ring on the jar and slide the oval
ring back over the hinge to hold it in place. Twist
the two ends of the coloured wire tightly together. ▶

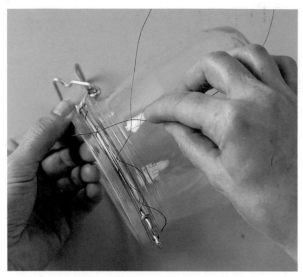

3 Make the first loop in the mesh by threading the wire under the hinge and through the first wrap around the ring, leaving a loop 1.5 cm/⅝ in deep. Repeat all round the jar to make 12 loops, keeping them equal in size.

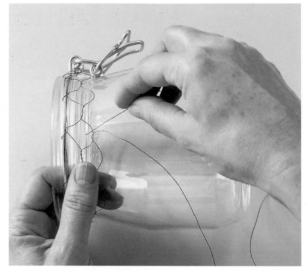

4 Wrap the coloured wire down one side of the loop directly under the hinge until you reach the mid point, then work round the jar to make a second row of loops, wrapping the wire twice through each loop in the previous row.

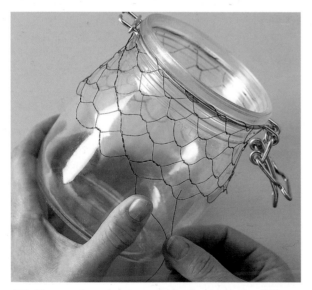

5 Repeat the pattern working down the jar. When you come to the end of the first length of wire, lay the end of a new length parallel with it and twist the ends together for about 2.5 cm/1 in.

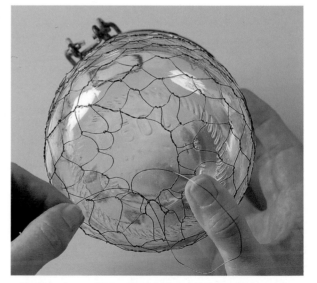

6 Continue the mesh for about 2.5 cm/1 in under the jar, then wrap the wire twice through each loop and pull it taut to draw the whole mesh tight. Wrap the wire all round the edges of the loops for a further round, then knot and trim the end.

TOOTHBRUSH HOLDER

A quirky design using coloured, plastic-coated wire makes a holder for a glass and four toothbrushes that will get you smiling in the morning. There are two wire loops behind the glass so that the frame can be screwed to the wall.

YOU WILL NEED
glass
1 mm/0.04 in plastic-coated steel wire
tape measure
wire cutters
5 mm/¼ in glass beads
pen
all-purpose instant glue

1 Select a glass that is wider at the top than the bottom. Cut a 1 m/3 ft length of wire and circle the glass with it, twisting the ends to secure.

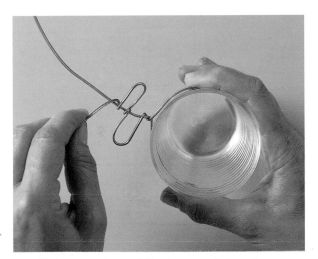

2 Twist one wire end firmly around the other, forming two loops on opposite sides as you do so.

3 Thread eight glass beads on to the straight wire and twist the second wire between them to hold them in place and create a solid spine. ▶

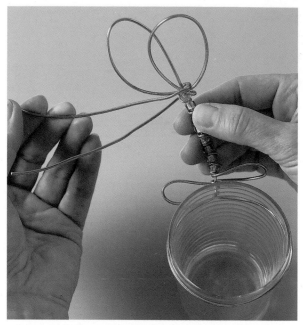

4 Form two loops with the ends of the wires to make a heart shape. Twist the ends together at the base of the heart and trim off any excess wire.

5 To make the toothbrush holders, cut two 30 cm/ 12 in lengths of wire and coil the central part of each one tightly around the circle.

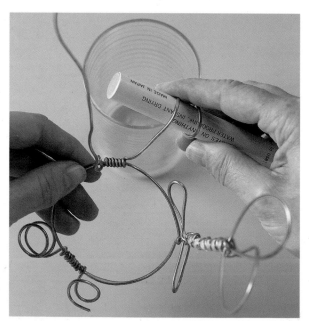

6 Coil the loose ends of the wires around a pen to make four small circles.

7 Add beads to the ends as a finishing touch, securing them with all-purpose instant glue.

JEWEL NIGHTLIGHT

This is an easy and effective way to create a magical container for a nightlight. When the candle is lit it looks like a little pile of treasure and gives a warm, sparkling light as a room decoration or on the table.

YOU WILL NEED
1.6 mm/0.06 in and 0.8 mm/0.03 in silver-plated wire
tape measure
wire cutters
large rolling pin
75 x 14 mm/⅝ in round glass beads
75 x 14 mm/⅝ in silver-plated bead cages
flat-nosed pliers
wooden spoon

Above: Because the silver-plated bead cages are shop-bought this striking piece is quick and easy to make.

1 Cut a 165 cm/65 in length of 1.6 mm/0.06 in silver-plated wire and coil it around a large rolling pin to make the frame.

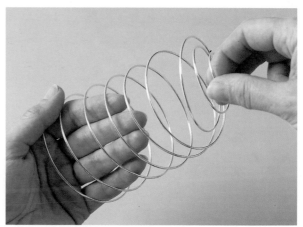

2 Slide the coil off the rolling pin and gently ease it apart a little. At one end, shape the frame into a peak by making the loops slightly smaller. Pull up the last couple of loops so that they sit upright.

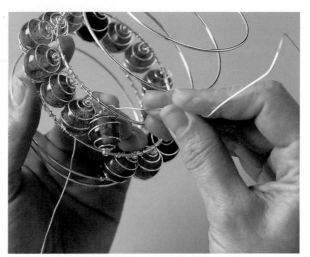

3 To put the glass beads inside the wire cages, pull each cage slightly apart and slip in a bead.

4 Leaving a loop of wire at the base for stability, begin binding the caged beads between the second and third loops, using 0.8 mm/0.03 in silver-plated wire. Pull the wire tight as you work, using flat-nosed pliers. Work around the loops until you reach the point where the coils are twisted upright. There should be approximately four rows of beads.

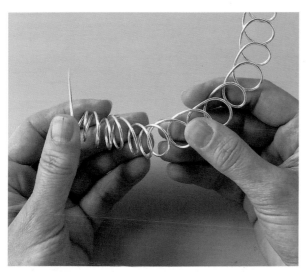

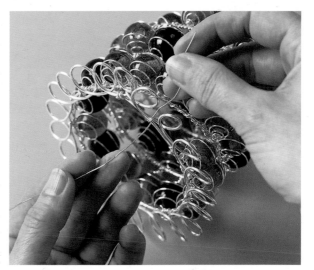

5 Wrap a 115 cm/45 in length of 1.6 mm/0.06 in silver-plated wire around the handle of a wooden spoon. Slide the coil off the handle, then pull out and flatten the loops to form a flat coil. Join the ends with a piece of fine wire to form the circular base.

6 Turn the frame upside down and attach the base to the lowest loop by wrapping fine wire around the base and the frame at three points.

▶

7 Finally, thread fine wire through the middle of a
bead and attach it to the top of the frame,
wrapping the wire around several times to secure.

WOVEN PIPE-CLEANER BASKET

This intriguing little basket is made using a simple wrapping technique. The tightly woven pipe cleaners give a softness that is irresistible to touch.

YOU WILL NEED
1.6 mm/0.06 in and 0.5 mm/0.02 in galvanized wire
tape measure
wire cutters
50 lilac and 24 grey 30 cm/12 in pipe cleaners
flat-nosed pliers
round-nosed pliers

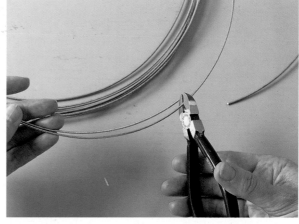

1 Measure and cut eight 36 cm/14 in lengths of 1.6 mm/0.06 in galvanized wire. Retain the curve of the wire as you cut the lengths from the coil. Cut a 30 cm/12 in length of 0.5 mm/0.02 in wire.

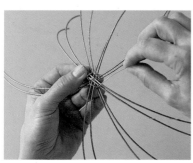

2 Use the fine wire to bind the struts together at the centre. Bind two pairs together at right angles, then place the remaining pairs diagonally. Wind the fine wire around the individual struts to hold them in position, evenly spaced.

3 Weave a lilac pipe cleaner over the centre of the basket so that all the fine wire is covered.

4 Take the pipe cleaner under each wire, back around it and then on to the next, pushing the pipe cleaners in towards the centre to keep the weave tight. Adjust the wires as necessary to keep the shape and spacing even. Work in lilac until the centre measures 7.5 cm/3 in. ▶

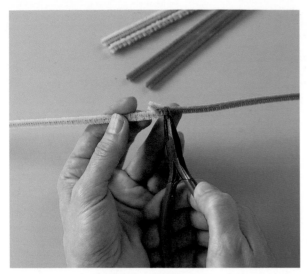

5 When you reach the end of a pipe cleaner or want to use a different colour, join the two lengths by bending a small hook in the end of each. Hook them together and flatten the hooks with flat-nosed pliers.

6 Work two rows in grey, then three lilac, two grey, four lilac, two grey, five lilac, and four grey, to bring you to the top edge.

7 Take two lilac pipe cleaners and hook them together, and do the same with two grey pipe cleaners. Hold the two colours together at one end and twist them firmly together.

8 Join the twisted length to the last grey length on the basket and lay it around the top edge, outside the wire struts. Trim the tops of the struts to 5 mm/ ¼ in and use round-nosed pliers to bend them over the "rope" edging. Weave the ends of the rope into its beginning.

FABRIC-COVERED BASKETS

These ingenious containers look like fat little pots, but are actually made of brightly coloured fabric stretched over simple wire frames. Use them for pot-pourri or cotton wool (cotton balls), or stand a small jar inside to hold a nightlight.

YOU WILL NEED
3 mm/0.11 in, 2 mm/0.08 in and 1 mm/0.04 in galvanized wire
tape measure
wire cutters
long-nosed pliers
masking tape
two-way stretch fabric
scissors
pins
sewing machine
matching thread
needle

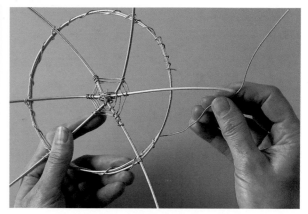

1 Measure and cut three 45 cm/18 in lengths of 3 mm/0.11 in galvanized wire. Cross the wires at the centres and bind together using 1 mm/ 0.04 in wire so that the prongs splay out evenly in a star shape. Using 2 mm/0.08 in wire, make a double ring 13 cm/5 in in diameter and bind it centrally to the framework to form a base.

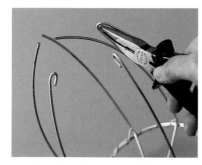

2 Bend each prong of the framework upwards where it joins the base to form the side of the container, then bend the end of each into a tight loop using long-nosed pliers.

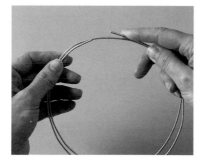

3 Make a second double ring of 2 mm/0.08 in wire to match the base, and hold the ends together temporarily using masking tape.

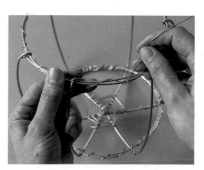

4 Slip the wire ring into the loops at the top of the framework, then bind in place using fine wire.

▶

5 Cut a 35 cm/15¾ in square of two-way stretch fabric. Fold in half and pin and stitch down one side, using a machine stretch stitch, to make a tube.

6 Turn the fabric tube right side out and place it inside the wire framework. Hand stitch the raw edge to the top ring.

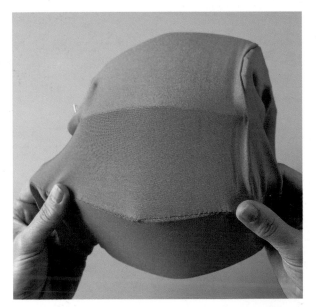

7 Pull the fabric up from inside the framework and carefully stretch it down around the outside of the tube.

8 Gather the raw edge under the base and stitch to the centre of the framework. Ease any remaining fabric up towards the top of the container, and secure with curly clips made from galvanized wire.

FESTIVE LIGHT BUSH

This pretty floral decoration will add sparkle to your Christmas table, but it would also create
a magical effect as temporary garden lighting for a party on a summer evening.

YOU WILL NEED

2 mm/0.08 in and 1 mm/0.04 in dark green plastic-coated
garden wire
tape measure
wire cutters
pliers
flower-shaped fairy(decorative) lights, 12v
broom handle
artificial leaves with wire stems
large pebble
flower pot
sand

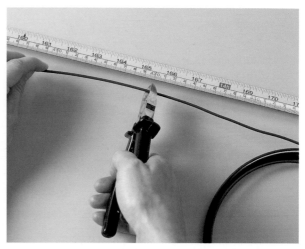

1 Cut a length of the thicker garden wire to match the length of the fairy (decorative) light flex (cord) and turn a loop in the end.

Above: White bulbs are the most elegant, but you could use differently coloured bulbs to match your colour scheme.

2 Bind the fairy (decorative) light flex (cord) to the thick wire using the finer wire. End the binding 20 cm/8 in beyond the last fairy (decorative) light.

3 Make coils in the wire by winding it around a broom handle.

4 At the end of the bound section, wrap the free end of the thick wire around a large stone.

5 Arrange the coiled wire in a bush shape. Support the coils by wiring them together, if necessary.

6 Attach the leaves at regular intervals by winding their stems around the coiled wire. ▶

7 Half-fill a pot with dry sand. Put in the stone, then support the plant stem with more sand.

8 Adjust the fairy (decorative) lights so that they are clear of the wires and the leaves.

FIESTA OIL BOTTLE

This jazzily coloured and beaded bottle is a perfect container for zesty salad dressings or olive oil. Its unique cover is made from the fine wires inside a telephone cable, whose stripes combine to create fascinating random patterns across the blocks of bold colour.

YOU WILL NEED
3 m/10 ft length of 6-pair telephone cable

empty thread reels

double-sided tape

tape measure

scissors

quarter wine bottle

small glass beads in two contrasting colours

a few larger glass beads

all-purpose instant glue

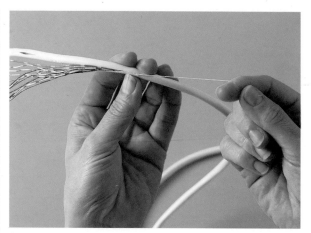

1 To extract the thin coloured wires from the cable, pull on the white cotton strand to strip back the plastic coating. Remove the wires, untwist them and roll each colour on to an empty reel. Choose six colours.

Above: A metal spout attached to a cork makes this vibrant bottle even more special.

2 Cut thin strips of double-sided tape and stick them in two lines down opposite sides of the bottle.

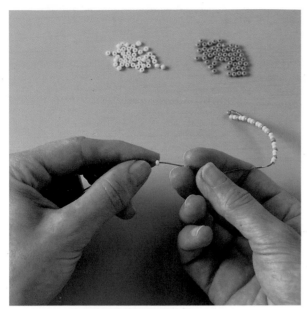

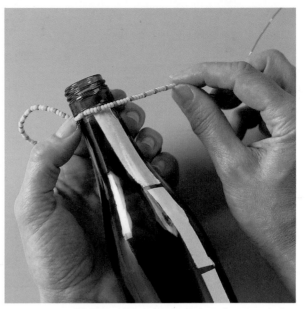

3 Before winding the first length of wire on to the bottle, thread on 6 cm/2½ in of small glass beads, using alternate colours. Form a loop.

4 Attach the loop to the bottle by twisting the wire back on itself. Thread on more beads to make a circle around the top.

5 Wind the remaining length of coloured wire around the bottle, threading on the odd small bead as you go. The adhesive tape will hold the wire in place.

6 To attach each new colour of wire, use a larger bead. Thread both wire ends through the bead and pull them downwards.

▶

7 Press the wire ends flat against the bottle and trim. Wind the new colour around the bottle as before, taking care to cover the loose ends securely.

8 Continue to wind the coloured wires down the length of the bottle, attaching new colours as you go. Stop attaching the small beads when you reach the main body of the bottle.

9 When you reach the bottom, thread another row of beads on to the last length of wire and glue this all round the bottle using all-purpose instant glue.

FLOWER HOLDER

Wire frameworks are essential to many flower arrangements and are usually intended to be unobtrusive, but this one is not only functional but decorative. Its organic-looking dark green curls make a characterful support for soft-stemmed flowers.

YOU WILL NEED

3 mm/0.11 in dark green plastic-coated garden wire
tape measure
wire cutters
flat-nosed pliers
broom handle
spray can
0.5 mm/0.02 in galvanized wire
bowl
pebbles

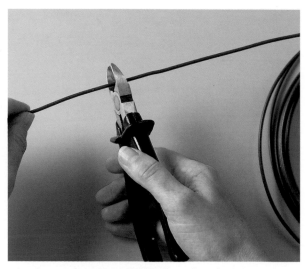

1 Cut eight 90 cm/35½ in lengths of garden wire to hold eight flowers stems.

Above: These bright orange gerberas go very well with the dark green wire. Tulips would look lovely, too.

2 Turn a loop in each end of each length to hide the raw end of the wire.

3 Just below each loop, wrap the wire three times around a broom handle to form the stem supports.

4 Using pliers, turn the stem through 90° under each coil, and open out the coils a little.

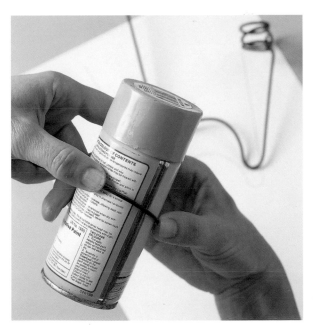

5 Create the final shape of the stem wire by using a spray can to form a curve at the end. Vary the heights of the flower supports.

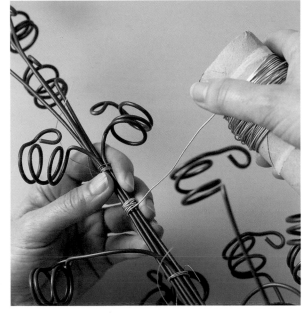

6 Gather all eight stems together and use fine galvanized wire to bind together the lower 8 cm/3¼ in of the long straight sections.

▶

7 Adjust the curved sections so that they are regularly spaced and weave the fine wire around the base curves and up the lower part of the outer flower supports to create a basket.

8 Place the basket in a suitable bowl and weight it with a ring of pebbles.

DESK ACCESSORIES

Organize your desk with this smart stationery set: the pen pot and note holder are fresh,
modern wire sculptures, and the notebook has a matching decoration on the front cover.
Complete the set with some original paper clips.

YOU WILL NEED
paper
pencil
2 mm/0.08 in, 3 mm/0.11 in and 1 mm/0.04 in galvanized wire
wire cutters
long-nosed pliers
tape measure
soldering iron, solder and flux
florist's wire
epoxy resin glue
hardback notebook
craft knife
cutting mat
bradawl (awl)
thick card (cardboard)

1 Trace and enlarge the templates at the back of the book for the spiral, triangle and flower shapes, then cut and bend lengths of 2 mm/0.08 in galvanized wire to match the designs.

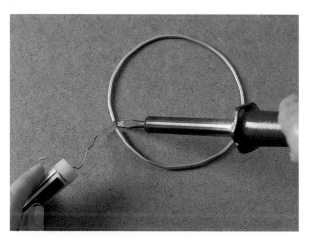

2 To make the pen holder, cut three 30 cm/12 in lengths of 3 mm/0.11 in galvanized wire and bend them into circles. Use a soldering iron to join the ends.

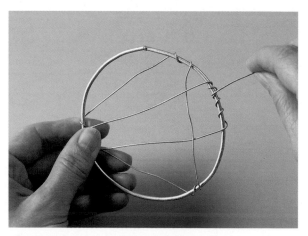

3 Stretch some lengths of florist's wire across the centre of one of the rings to form the foundations for the base of the pen holder.

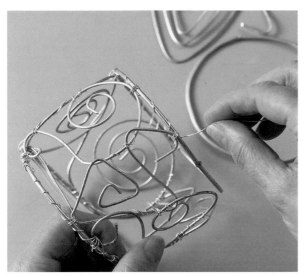

4 Using wire, bind several wire shapes to the base ring and to each other to form the sides. Bind on another ring and repeat. Add the third ring to make the top and cut out and insert a circle of thick card (cardboard) in the bottom. Repeat for the note holder, making two squares for the top and base.

5 To make a paper clip, cut a 35 cm/14 in length of 3 mm/0.11 in wire and bend one end to match one of the template shapes, then bend t he remaining wire back on itself behind the original shape.

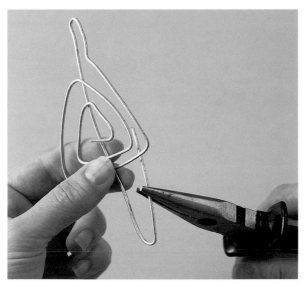

6 Bend the remaining end back on itself as shown to form a large paper clip.

7 For the notebook, use a craft knife to cut a square from the front cover of a hardback notebook. Pierce a small hole halfway along each side of the window using a bradawl (awl). ▶

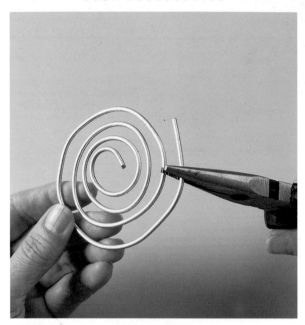

8 Bend a length of 3 mm/0.11 in wire into a
spiral shape to fit the window in the book cover.
Stick a sheet of coloured paper to the inside of
the cover.

9 Place the spiral inside the window, then bind it
to the book using florist's wire.

GARDEN DRINKS CARRIER

Instead of balancing them precariously on a tray, a bottle and glasses can be safely carried
into the garden in this stylish and sturdy carrier made of wire and bamboo.

YOU WILL NEED
green bamboo canes
tape measure
saw
skewer or length of thick wire
2 mm/0.08 in and 1 mm/0.04 in galvanized wire
wire cutters
broom handle
flat-nosed pliers
food can
3.5 mm/0.14 in plastic-coated garden wire
fine wire
length of plastic tubing (aquarium air line)

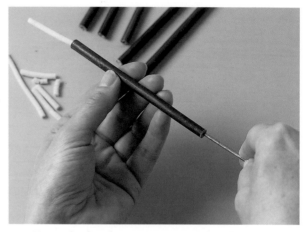

1 From the bamboo canes, cut eight 15 cm/6 in
lengths for the base and eight 17 cm/6¾ in
lengths for the uprights. Use a skewer to remove the
pith from the centre of each.

2 To make each glass carrier, use the broom handle
to turn a loop in the end of a length of 2 mm/
0.08 in galvanized wire. Bend the short end to lie
against the length and thread both ends of the wire
through one of the base canes.

3 Measure 8 cm/3¼ in along the wire from the end
of the cane, and at this point form a circle
around a can. Twist the end around the wire to
secure, and cut off the excess. Repeat with the other
base canes to make eight sections.

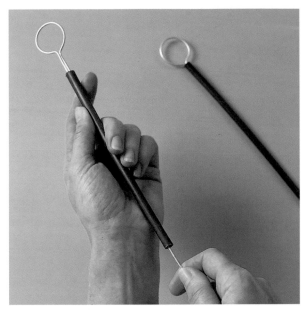

4 Make eight more looped wire lengths and thread them through the upright canes.

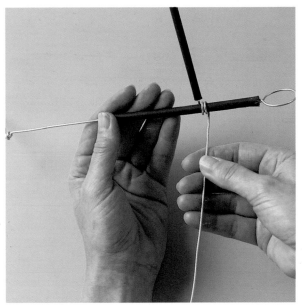

5 Use the end of the wire to bind each upright cane to a base cane, 8 cm/3¼ in from the end with the small loop, and trim.

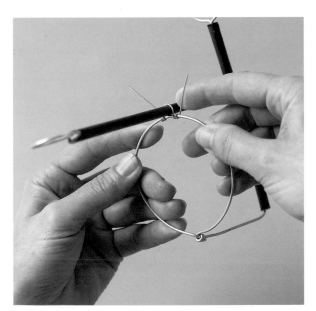

6 Make two 90° bends in each long wire, one at the end of the base cane and the other before the ring, and bind the ring to the upright with a short length of fine wire.

7 When the eight sections are completed, arrange them in a circle, laying down each pair of opposites together. Using fine wire, bind all the central loops together and bind the rings to each other. ▶

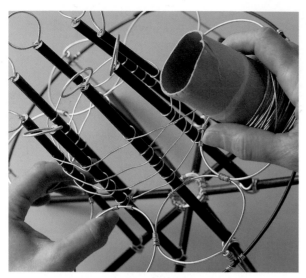

8 Cut a length of plastic-coated garden wire to fit around the outside of the carrier and twist the ends to make a circle. Use fine wire to bind this in place just under each ring, and to bind the upright canes together.

9 Turn the carrier upside down and loop fine wire around the base canes to make a platform for the glasses.

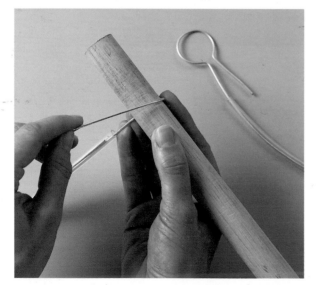

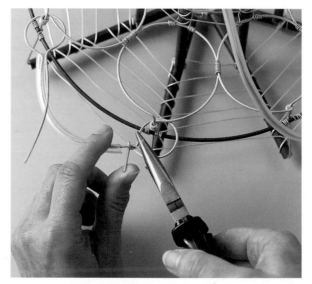

10 To make the carrying handles use the broom handle to form a loop in the ends of two short and two long lengths of wire and thread the wire into two lengths of plastic tubing. Form a second loop at the other end of the lengths of wire.

11 Thread the loops of the long carrying handles through the loops at the top of the uprights, then secure them by twisting the ends of the wires around the handles. Attach the two short handles around the base rings in the same way.

DECORATIVE SHELVES

These semicircular copper shelves have a Spanish style and will look good anywhere, whether you make just one or a group to hold plants or ornaments. The flattened coil edging lends strength to the framework as well as creating a shallow lip to stop anything from slipping off.

YOU WILL NEED
paper
felt-tipped pen
2 mm/0.08 in, 1.6 mm/0.06 in and 0.5 mm/0.02 in copper wire
tape measure
wire cutters
flat-nosed pliers
round-nosed pliers
masking tape
30 cm/12 in length of 1 cm/½ in wooden dowel
two picture hooks and nails

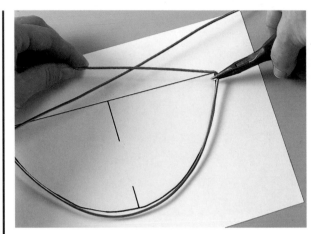

1 Enlarge the template at the back of the book to a width of 18 cm/7 in. Cut an 80 cm/32 in length of 2 mm/0.08 in copper wire and use the template as a guide to form the shelf frame, starting with the centre of the wire at the centre front.

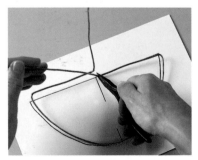

2 At the centre back, bend a right angle in the two ends of the wire so that they are vertical and parallel with each other. These will form the struts under the shelf.

3 Using a pair of round-nosed pliers, turn each end of the wire to form a 5 mm/¼ in out-ward-facing hook.

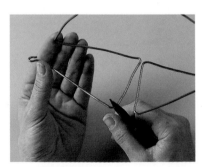

4 Measure 6 cm/2¾ in along the struts from the base and bend them out to the sides, so that the hooks meet the back corners of the base. Attach the hooks and close them firmly.

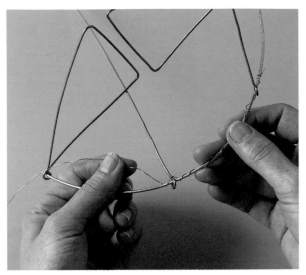

5 Cut two 23 cm/9 in lengths of 2 mm/0.08 in wire and form a hook in one end of each. Attach these to the outer curved frame one-third of the way in from each side and close the hooks firmly. To hold them in place, wrap a length of 0.5 mm/0.02 in wire along the front edge and around both hooks.

6 Bring both wires back to the centre of the back edge and bend them up at right angles so that they run parallel to the two central support wires.

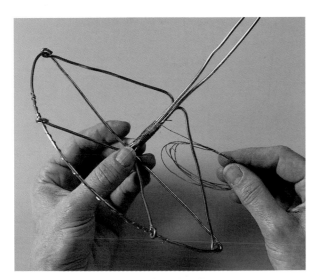

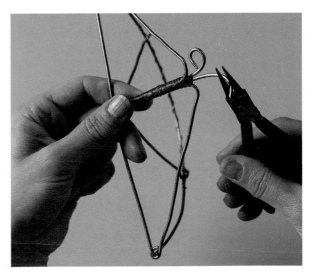

7 Cut a 150 cm/59 in length of 0.5 mm/0.02 in wire and bind the four lengths of wire tightly together with close coils. When you reach the bottom, trim the wire leaving a 2.5 cm/1 in tail and use pliers to tuck it back up under the coils to secure it.

8 Trim the two wire ends at the bottom to 4 cm/1½ in and use round-nosed pliers to bend them into outward-facing loops which will lie flush against the wall.

▶

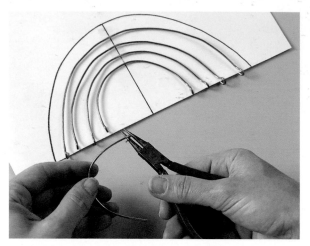

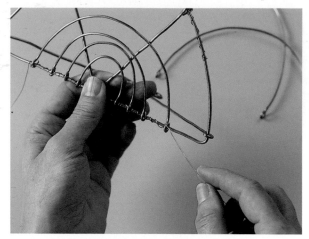

9 Make the wire hoops for the shelf using 1.6 mm/ 0.06 in wire. Turn a hook in one end then bend the wire in a semicircle 1 cm/½ in in from the edge of the template and finish with a hook at the other end. Tape this piece of wire in place and repeat, working inwards in 1 cm/½ in steps to make six semicircles.

10 Wrap a 60 cm/24 in length of 0.5 mm/ 0.02 in wire once around the centre back struts. Hook the smallest semicircle of wire into position on the back edge and firmly close the hooks. Wrap the fine wire around it to hold it in place, then repeat to attach the other semicircles. Fasten off the fine wire tightly at the corners.

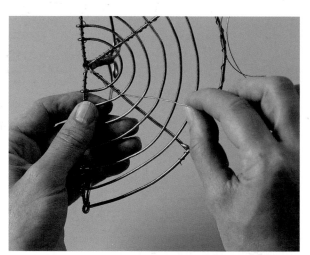

11 Using fine wire, attach the semicircles to the shelf supports in the same way, working in along one support and back out along the other.

12 Cut a 120 cm/47 in length of 1.6 mm/0.06 in wire, and wrap it around a length of 1 cm/½ in dowel to make a flattened coil. Pull out the coil so that it stretches evenly around the curved outside edge of the shelf, and bind it in place with a 60 cm/24 in length of 0.5 mm/0.02 in wire. Hang the shelf using a picture hook in each corner.

PANELLED FLOWER POT COVER

*Fan-shaped panels of opaque polypropylene are the perfect foil for the light,
silvery wire framework around this pot. An original decorative feature is the wire stitching
used to attach the plastic to the framework.*

YOU WILL NEED

flower pot, base circumference 33 cm/13 in, height 15 cm/6 in
paper
pencil
ruler
scissors
polypropylene sheet
long-nosed pliers
2 mm/0.08 in, 3 mm/0.11 in and 1 mm/0.04 in galvanized wire
wire cutters
bradawl (awl)
cutting mat
soldering iron, solder and flux

1 Use the template to make a pattern to fit exactly around the outside of your pot. If your pot is not the specified size, adjust the template accordingly.

Above: If you prefer, you could use your own design for the four wire panels.

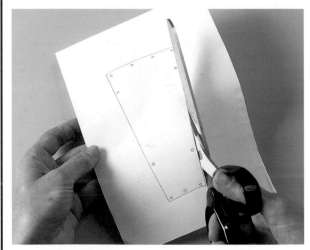

2 Make another template showing the stitching holes for the plastic panels. Cut out.

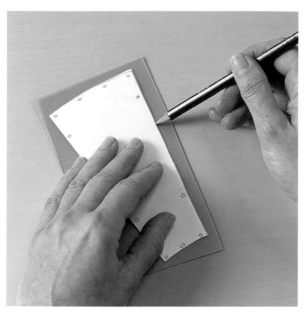

3 Using a soft pencil, trace around the template on to the polypropylene sheet. Cut out four identical pieces.

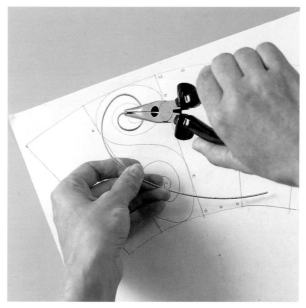

4 Using pliers, curl a piece of 2 mm/0.08 in wire to match the S-shape design. Repeat to make four matching S-shapes.

5 Pierce small holes around the edges of the plastic panels where indicated on the template, using a bradawl.

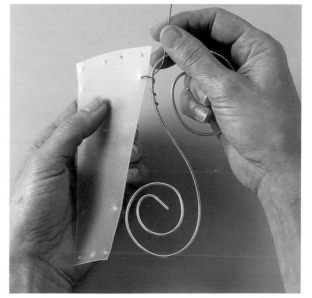

6 Using 1 mm/0.04 in wire, bind the wire S-shapes to the plastic sections. Join all four plastic sections together in this way with a wire shape between each one. ▶

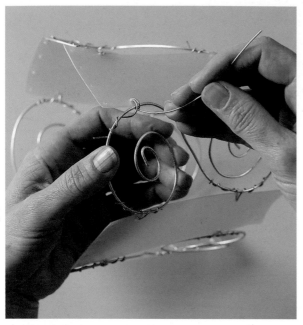

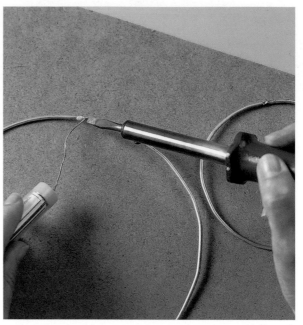

7 Bind the last panels and wire shape together to complete the pot shape.

8 Cut two lengths of 3 mm/0.11 in wire to fit around the top and the base of the pot cover. Solder the ends of each length together.

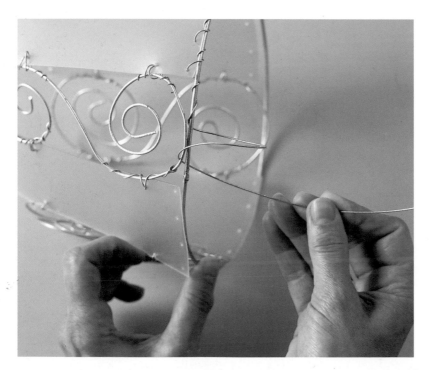

9 Bind the top and bottom rings to the pot cover using the fine galvanized wire. Place the flower pot in the cover.

PICTURE FRAME

This imposing little frame is made from nothing more substantial than cardboard, wire and some metallic paint, yet it looks weighty and solid, and even has its own wire stand.

YOU WILL NEED

paper

pencil

2 mm/0.08 in, 3 mm/0.11 in and 1 mm/0.04 in galvanized wire

tape measure

wire cutters

long-nosed pliers

soldering iron, solder and flux

thick card (cardboard)

craft knife

steel ruler

cutting mat

double-sided adhesive tape

bradawl (awl)

silver metallic paint

paint brush

epoxy resin adhesive

1 Trace the template at the back of the book. Cut four 70 cm/28 in lengths of 2 mm/0.08 in wire and, using long-nosed pliers, bend each length to match the spiral and zig-zag shapes along one side of the frame.

2 Cut ten 30 cm/12 in lengths of 2 mm/0.08 in wire and curl each one into a tight S-shape.

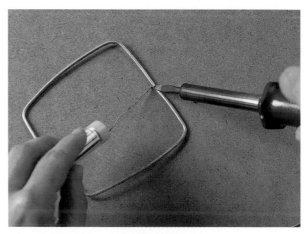

3 Cut a 40 cm/16 in length of 3 mm/0.11 in wire and bend into a square to form the centre of the picture frame, arranging the ends in the middle of one side. Solder the ends together.

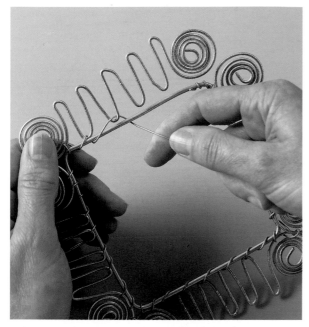

4 Using 1 mm/0.04 in wire, bind the four side sections to the central frame.

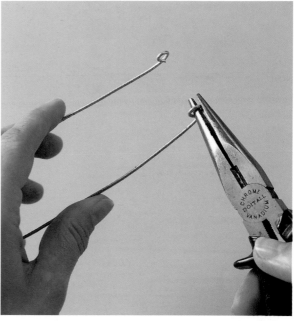

5 To make the stand, bend a 30 cm/12 in length of 2 mm/0.08 in wire into a narrow U-shape, then curl each end into a tight loop using flat-nosed pliers.

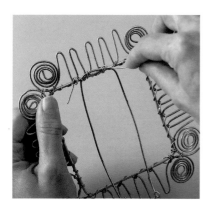

6 Using 1 mm/0.04 in wire, bind the stand centrally to the back of the top of the frame.

7 Cut two pieces of thick card (cardboard) to fit the frame, using a craft knife and steel ruler. Cut a "window" out of the front section and a slightly larger window from the back section. Reserve the central part of the back. Stick the frames together using double-sided tape.

8 Using a bradawl (awl), pierce a small hole in each corner of the picture holder. Paint the front section silver.

▶

9 Bind the picture holder to the frame at each corner using short lengths of fine wire.

10 Use epoxy resin adhesive to glue the small S-shapes around the front of the frame. Insert the picture and replace the reserved cardboard square to hold it in place.

MATERIALS

Buy wire from jewellery, craft and sculpture suppliers as well as hardware stores and specialist wire and electrical suppliers.

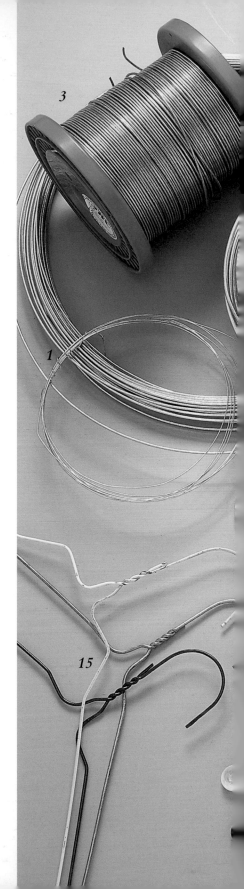

ALUMINIUM WIRE
This extremely soft wire is sometimes available in anodized colours. It does not conduct heat well and can be difficult to solder.

COPPER WIRE
To keep the sheen on this soft wire, spray the completed project lightly with clear lacquer.

ELECTRICAL AND TELEPHONE CABLE
Strip off the plastic insulation around electrical cable to reveal up to 12 plastic-covered wires.

ENAMELLED COPPER WIRE
This soft wire is available in fine gauges in a range of colours, and is excellent for decorative effects.

FLORIST'S WIRE
Use this soft, fine-gauged wire for wrapping over wires to add strength or to bind wires together.

GARDEN WIRE
Plastic–coated garden wire is weather-proof, soft and easy to work with.

GALVANIZED WIRE
This is a strong, steel wire that does not rust. Clean off the grease coating before soldering.

PIPE CLEANERS
Sometimes called chenille stems, pipe cleaners come in a fantastic variety of colours.

POLYPROPYLENE
Polypropylene is a strong, heat-resistant, weather-proof material available from specialist (specialty) stationery suppliers.

PLASTIC-COATED STEEL WIRE
Take care not to split the plastic coating when bending and twisting this wire.

SILVER-PLATED WIRE
This attractive wire must be sprayed with clear lacquer to prevent it from tarnishing.

WIRE COAT HANGERS
Although strong and durable, these are not easy to bend and are only suitable for the simplest forms.

Opposite: galvanized wire (1), garden wire (2), aluminium wire (3), plastic–coated steel wire (4), electrical and telephone cable (5), enamelled copper wire (6), copper wire (7), pipe cleaners (8), plastic tubing (9), bamboo (10), polypropylene (11), plastic mesh (12), paper (13), beads (14), wire coat hangers (15), silver-plated wire (16), florist's wire (17), bead cages (18).

EQUIPMENT

The most important tools for wirework are a good pair of wire cutters and pliers for manipulating the wire accurately.

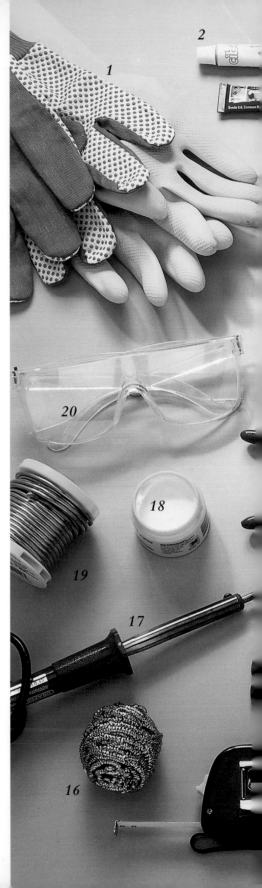

BRADAWL (AWL)
Use this tool for punching holes into papers, plastics and some soft metals.

CROCHET HOOK, KNITTING AND SEWING NEEDLES
Fine-gauge wires can be used for sewing, crocheting or knitting.

DOWEL, ROLLING PIN AND WOODEN SPOONS
Wrap wire around any of these items to make a range of coil sizes.

EPOXY RESIN GLUE
For a strong bond, use two-part epoxy resin glue to attach wire to another material.

GLOVES AND GOGGLES
It is a good idea to wear gardening or household gloves to prevent damage to the hands, and goggles to protect the eyes as small bits of wire can shoot out while cutting.

PLIER (LOCKING) WRENCH
Use this to hold several strands of wire together at one end when plaiting (braiding) or twisting.

PLIERS
Flat-nosed pliers usually have a spring action and should have flat, smooth inner surfaces.

Round-nosed pliers are essential for making hook and loop shapes in wire.

Long-nosed, or needle-nosed pliers have a serrated surface on the inside of the nose and often have a cutting jaw. Take care not to mark soft wires when using them.

SOLDERING EQUIPMENT
Electric or gas-canister soldering irons may be used for working with wires. Solder is essential for making a strong permanent bond. Flux helps the solder flow smoothly over the heated area.

WIRE CUTTERS
The heavier the cutters, the heavier the gauge of wire they will cut. Wire nippers are good for very soft or fine-gauge wires.

Opposite: gloves (1), epoxy resin glue (2), snipe nosed pliers (3), wire strippers (4), craft knife (5), crochet hook (6), wooden spoon (7), rolling pins (8), dowels (9), knitting needles (10), tape (11), bradawls (awls) (12), plier wrench (13), scissors (14), tape measure (15), wire scrubber (16), soldering iron (17), flux (18), solder (19), goggles (20), round-nosed pliers (21), long-nosed pliers (22), flat-nosed pliers (23), spiralling tool (24), wire cutters (25)

BASIC TECHNIQUES

It is worth practising these techniques, as most of the projects use at least one or two of them.

COILS AND FLATTENED COILS

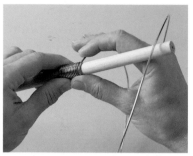

1 Choose a dowel, or other cylindrical object of a suitable size. Hold one end of the wire tight to the side of the dowel with your thumb and wrap tightly down the length of the dowel. Use pliers, if necessary, to coil the ends of the wire around the dowel.

2 Before removing the wire, push the coils tightly together, then slide them off.

3 Hold the coil firmly and pull it open, working your way up the length of the tight coil, to achieve an even spacing.

4 You can flatten a large coil, or one that is made from soft wire, with your fingers. Begin at the top end and simply push the coil flat, using pressure from your thumb and forefinger on either side.

5 To flatten small coils or coils made from harder wires, use a rolling pin. Lay the slightly opened coil on a piece of folded cloth. Starting at the end closest to you, push the rolling pin slowly along the length of the coil. As it flattens out the coil will curve, but this can be corrected by hand.

6 Use your thumb and fore-finger to spread the flat coils open if required. Work from one end to the other, keeping the spacing between the coil loops even.

SPIRALS

To use this technique you will need two large metal washers, a bolt to fit loosely into the holes in the washers and two nuts to fit the bolt.

1 Screw one nut on to the bolt almost to the top, and add a washer. Take a length of wire and use flat-nosed pliers to make a right angle bend near the end. Thread this bent end into the hole in the washer beside the bolt.

2 Place the second washer and second nut on the bolt and screw the nut down so that the wire fits tightly between the washers.

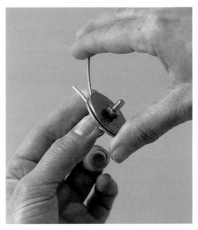

3 Grasping the tail end of wire from the centre hole with one hand, bend the rest of the wire hard around the bolt.

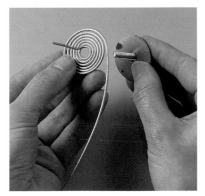

4 Remove one of the nuts and the washer. Slide the spiral off the bolt.

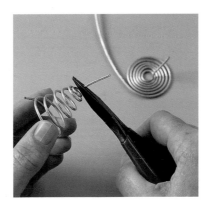

5 To make a conical spiral, grasp hold of the tail of wire with flat-nosed pliers and pull the spiral gently out to the length you want. Use wire cutters to cut off the tail in the centre of the spiral.

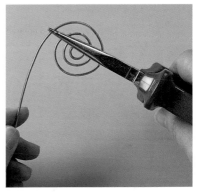

6 Larger, looser spirals can easily be made by hand. Form a closed loop in one end of the wire using round-nosed pliers. Use long-nosed pliers to hold the shape of the spiral as you loosely wind the wire around, keeping the spacing even.

TWISTING

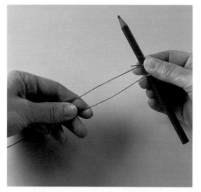  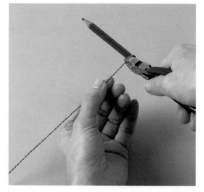

1 Fold a length of wire in half. Wrap the two cut ends around the middle of a pencil three times, to hold them in place, and slip another pencil into the looped end.

2 Begin twisting the two pencils in opposite directions. Continue until the twisted pattern is to your liking.

3 To remove the wire, cut off the ends near the pencil using a wire cutter. To twist two colours together, cut both to the same length and wrap the ends around pencils at both ends.

PLAITING (BRAIDING)

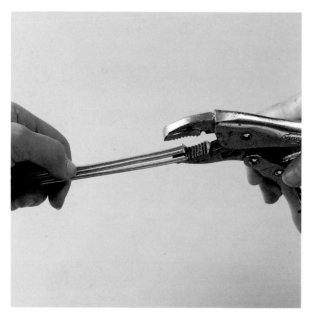 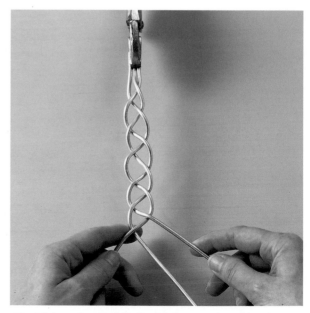

1 Cut three equal lengths of wire, and use a plier wrench or other clamping tool to hold the three strands together at the top.

2 Make a loose plait (braid) by crossing the wires from alternate sides to the centre in succession, to the end of the length. You will need to wrap the ends of the wires to hold the plait (braid) together.

SOLDERING

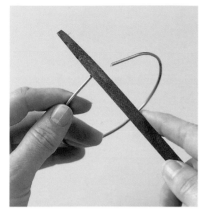  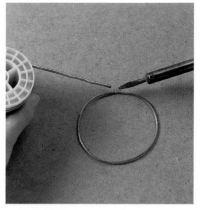

1 If you are soldering wire ends together, use a metal file to file the cut ends flat. Some wires have a greasy protective coating that will hinder soldering, so clean the area with a wire scrubber and some soapy water.

2 Lay the two pieces of wire, with ends butted together, on a protected surface. Heat the area to be joined using the soldering iron. Using a fine piece of wire or wood, spread a small amount of flux over the join.

3 Touch the tip of a length of solder to the join and heat with the soldering iron until it has melted and flowed into place along the join. Leave to cool before touching.

MAKING HOOKS

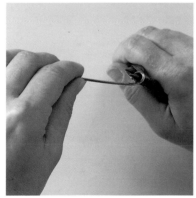  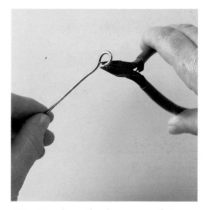

1 Use round-nosed pliers to grip the end of a length of wire. Grip the wire at the base of the pliers for a large hook, or at the tip for a small one. Hold the loose end of the wire with one hand and turn the pliers to bend the wire into a loop.

2 Grip the loop near its base and bend it back. This will make the loop open up.

3 To close the loop, use flat-nosed pliers to tighten the open end against the length of wire.

TEMPLATES

Enlarge the templates on a photocopier, or trace the design and draw a grid of evenly spaced squares over your tracing. Draw a larger grid on to another piece of paper and copy the outline square by square. Draw over the lines to make sure they are continuous.

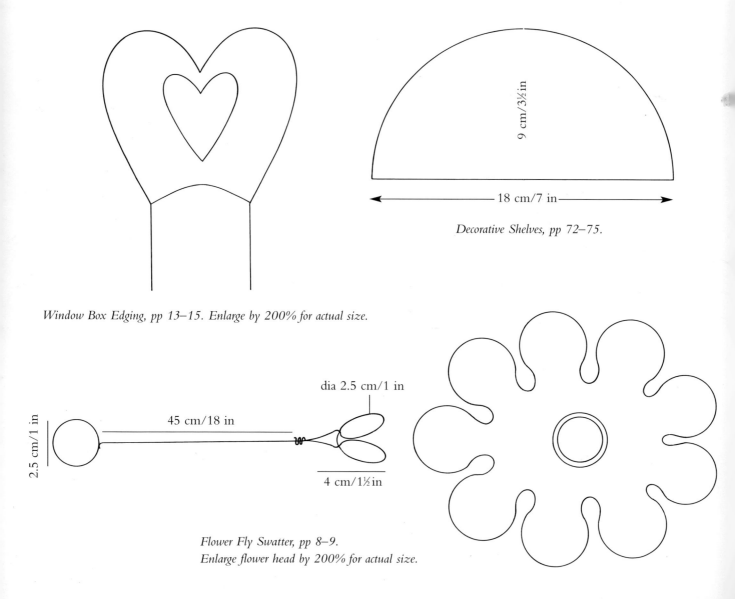

9 cm/3½ in

18 cm/7 in

Decorative Shelves, pp 72–75.

Window Box Edging, pp 13–15. Enlarge by 200% for actual size.

dia 2.5 cm/1 in

45 cm/18 in

2.5 cm/1 in

4 cm/1½ in

Flower Fly Swatter, pp 8–9.
Enlarge flower head by 200% for actual size.

Desk Accessories, pp 64–67. Enlarge by 200% for actual size.

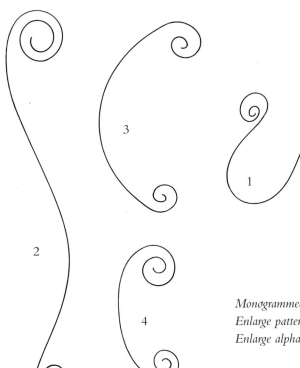

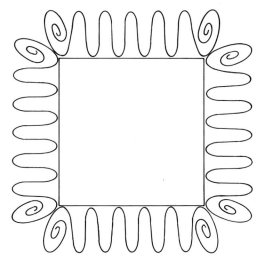

Picture Frame, pp 80–83.
Enlarge by 200% for actual size.

Monogrammed Clothes Hanger, pp 32–35.
Enlarge patterns inside hanger by 200% for actual size.
Enlarge alphabet by 350% for actual size.

A B C D E F G H I J K L M

N O P Q R S T U V W X Y Z

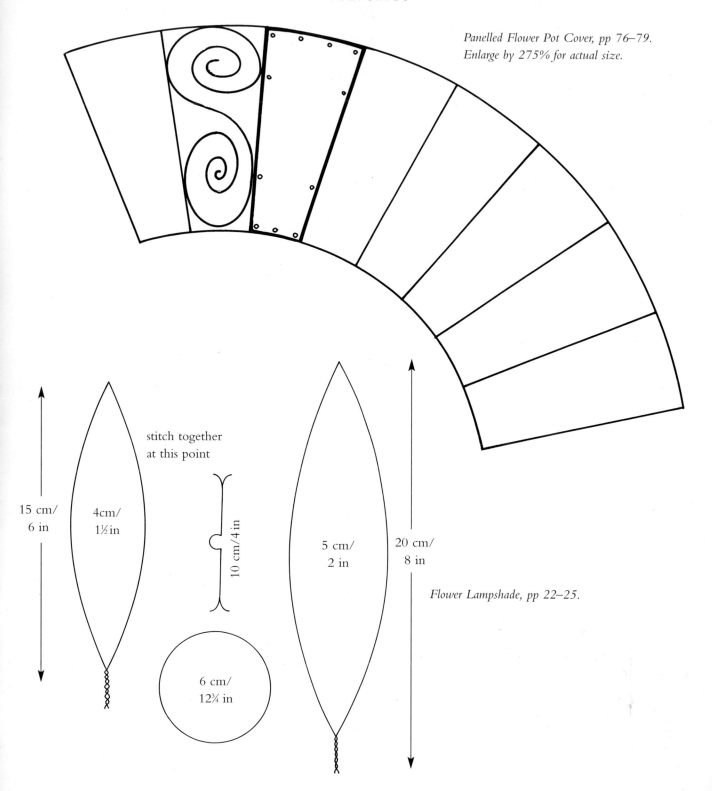

Panelled Flower Pot Cover, pp 76–79.
Enlarge by 275% for actual size.

stitch together
at this point

15 cm/
6 in

4cm/
1½ in

10 cm/4 in

5 cm/
2 in

20 cm/
8 in

6 cm/
12¾ in

Flower Lampshade, pp 22–25.

SUPPLIERS

The specialist materials and equipment that you will require for the wireworks projects featured in this book are available from any good art supply shop.

UNITED KINGDOM
The Bead Shop
21a Tower Street
London
WC1
tel: 020 7240 0931

J. W. Bollom
15 Theobalds Road
London
WC1X 8SN
tel: 020 7242 0313
fax: 020 7831 2457

Craft Depot
Somerton Business Park
Somerton
Somerset
TA11 6SB
tel: 01458 274727
fax: 01458 272932

Maplin Electronics plc
186 Edgware Road
W2 6DS
tel: 020 7723 6641
www.maplin.co.uk

Scientific Wire Company
18 Raven Road
London
E18 1HW
tel: 020 8505 0002
fax: 020 8559 1114
www.wires.co.uk

Alec Tiranti
Sculptors' Tools & Materials
70 High Street
Theale
RG7 5AR
tel: 0118 930 2775
www.tiranti.co.uk

USA
Are, Inc.
P.O. Box 8
Greensboro
UT 05842
tel: 802 533 7007

Art Supply Warehouse
5325 Departure Drive
North Raleigh, NC 27616
tel: 919 878 5077
www.aswexpress.com

Craft Catalogue
P.O. Box 1069
Reynoldsburg, OH 43068
tel: 800 777 1442

Craft King
P.O. Box 90637
Lakeland, FL 33804
tel: 800 769 9494
www.craft-king.com

CANADA
Abbey Arts & Crafts
4118 East Hastings Street
Vancouver, B.C.
tel: 604 229 5201

Lewiscraft
2300 Yonge Street
Toronto
Ontario M4P 1EA
tel: 416 483 2783

ACKNOWLEDGEMENTS

The publishers would like to thank the following people for designing the projects in this book: Andrew Gillmore for the projects on pp 8–9, 27–28, 52–55 and 68–71. Jennie Russell for the projects on pp10–12, 39–41 and 56–63. Karin Hossack for the projects on pp13–16, 19–21, 29–31, 37–38, 47–48 and 72–75. Sue Radcliffe for the projects on pp17–18, 22–26, 32–36 and 42–46. Alison Jenkins for the projects on pp49–51, 64–67, 76–79 and 80–83.

INDEX